WORKBOOKS

K Science

Author Hugh Westrup

Educational Consultant Kara Pranikoff

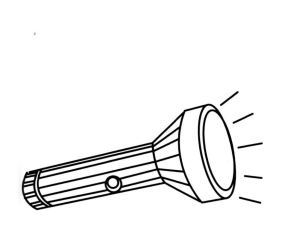

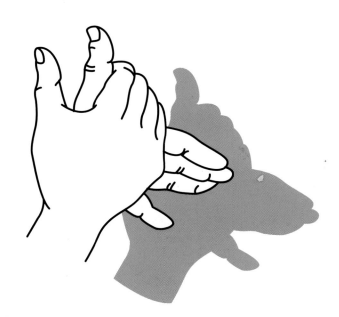

DK | Penguin Random House

US Editor Nancy Ellwood
US Educational Consultant Kara Pranikoff
Managing Art Editor Richard Czapnik
Senior Editors Fran Baines, Cécile Landau
Art Director Martin Wilson
Pre-production Francesca Wardell

DK Delhi
Asst. Editor Nishtha Kapil
Asst. Art Editors Tanvi Nathyal, Yamini Panwar
DTP Designer Anita Yadav
Dy. Managing Editor Soma B. Chowdhury

First American Edition, 2014
Published in the United States by DK Publishing
1450 Broadway, New York, New York 10018

19 10 9 8 7 6 5 4 3
010–197330–01/14

Copyright © 2014 Dorling Kindersley Limited

A catalog record for this book is
available from the Library of Congress
ISBN: 978-1-4654-1727-5

DK books are available at special discounts when purchased in bulk
for sales promotions, premiums, fund-raising, or educational use.
For details, contact:
DK Publishing Special Markets
1450 Broadway, New York, New York 10018
SpecialSales@dk.com.

Printed and bound in China

All images © Dorling Kindersley Limited
For further information see: www.dkimages.com

A WORLD OF IDEAS:
SEE ALL THERE IS TO KNOW
www.dk.com

Contents

This chart lists all the topics
in the *book*.

A garden is a small piece of land where flowers, fruits, and vegetables are grown. Some animals live in a garden, too.

Can you find the animals living in the garden?
Point to each animal and name it.

A plant has many parts to help it grow.

Find each part of the plant and say its name.

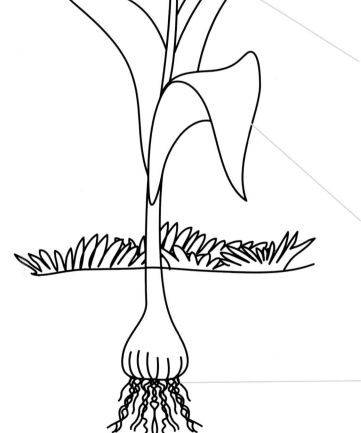

This plant is a tulip.

The flower is where the seeds are made so that new plants can grow.

The stem of the tulip brings water to all the parts of the plant.

The leaves take in sunlight for the plant so it can make food.

The roots of the tulip grow in the ground and help the plant get water.

FACTS

A tree is a large plant. The stem of a tree is made out of wood.

Touch each part of the tree and say its name.

This tree has many of the same parts as the tulip plant you saw on page 5.

The leaves take in sunlight for the plant so it can make food.

The branches of the tree stretch up to the sky so that the leaves can get lots of sunlight.

The stem of the tree is made of wood. It is called the trunk. The trunk brings water to all the parts of the plant.

The roots of the tree grow in the ground and help the tree get water.

Some trees lose their leaves in the fall and grow new leaves in the spring. Trees that lose their leaves are called deciduous trees.

During the summer, deciduous trees have all their leaves. During the fall, the leaves of deciduous trees fall to the ground. During the winter, you only see the branches of a deciduous tree. During the spring, the leaves grow back. Point to each tree and name the season it is in.

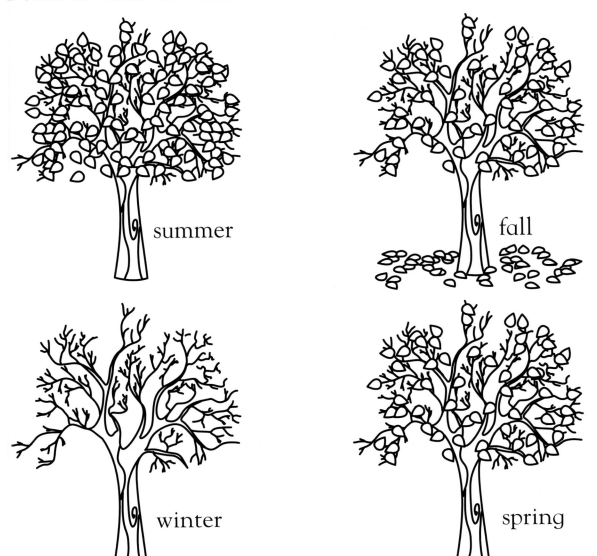

summer

fall

winter

spring

FACTS

Many foods that we eat are plants.

Point to the two plants that we eat, and name them.

apple

tulip

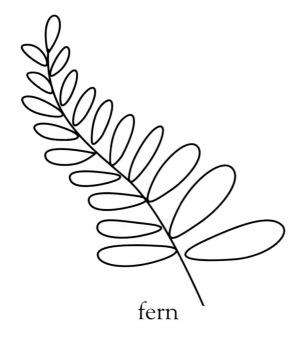

fern

tomato

Vegetables come from different parts of plants.

The roots of a plant grow in the ground and help the plant get water. Carrots and potatoes are root vegetables. The stem of the plant brings water to all the parts of the plant. Asparagus and celery are stems. The leaves take in sunlight for the plant so it can make food. Spinach and lettuce are leaf vegetables.

Point to each vegetable below, and say its name.
Is it a root, stem, or leaf vegetable?

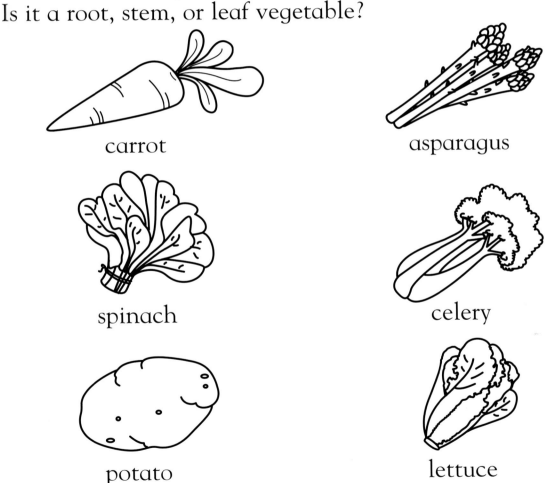

carrot

asparagus

spinach

celery

potato

lettuce

FACTS

A fruit is the part of a plant that contains seeds.

Circle the fruit in each picture.

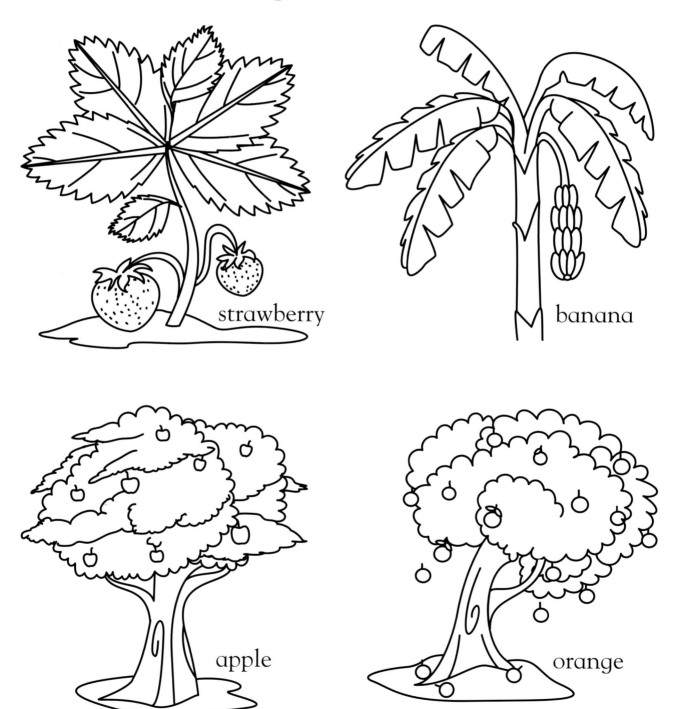

strawberry

banana

apple

orange

Many things we use are made from plants and trees.

Connect each plant with the things that are made from it.

sock

This is a cotton plant. Many things that you wear are made from cotton. Socks and T-shirts are often made from cotton.

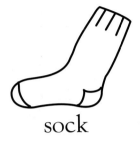

book

t-shirt

This is a tree. Many things you use every day are made from the wood of trees. Baseball bats and books are made from trees.

baseball bat

Plants need water to grow.

TEST

What You Need:

paper towel   2 plastic bags

water

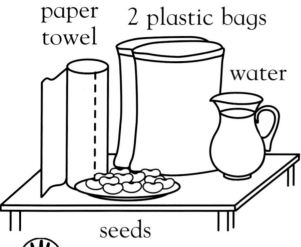

seeds

 **What To Do:**

1. Place some bean seeds on a wet paper towel and fold it over. Place the paper towel in bag 1 and seal it.

2. Place some bean seeds on a dry paper towel and fold it over. Place the paper towel in bag 2 and seal it.

3. Put both bags in a warm, light place.

RESULT

After a week, open the bags. Describe what has happened to the seeds. Circle the picture that looks like the bag with water. Put an **X** on the picture that looks like the bag without water.

bag with wet seeds

bag with dry seeds

Plants need light to grow.

TEST

What You Need:

two seedlings of the same type of plant of equal size

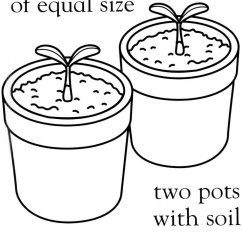

two pots with soil

 **What To Do:**

1. Plant each seedling in a pot of soil.

2. Put one pot in a dark place.

3. Put the other pot in a sunny place.

4. Check the plants every day for one week and water them if necessary.

RESULT

Watch the growth of the plants for a week. Describe what has happened to the plants. Circle the picture that looks like the plant that got sun. Put an **X** on the picture of the plant that was in the dark.

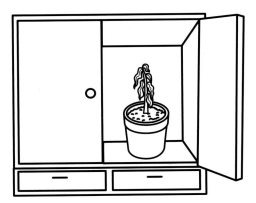

Seeds need to travel to different places to grow new plants. They travel to find a place that has light and water.

Seeds travel in many ways. Match the seeds to the way they travel.

strawberry

These seeds have a parachute of fine hairs. They are carried by the wind.

acorn

The hooks of this seed stick to the fur of animals passing by.

dandelion

These seeds are eaten with fruit, pass through the animal, and grow in a new place.

burr

Squirrels bury these seeds to eat in the winter.

FACTS

A mountain is land that rises high above the ground around it. Mountains are made of soil and rocks. Trees grow on some mountains. Very high mountains can be covered in snow.

The animals in the picture live in the mountains. Can you name them all? Color the picture.

An ocean is a large body of water. Ocean water is salty. Many animals live in the ocean.

Draw a picture of an animal that lives in the ocean. Then color the picture.

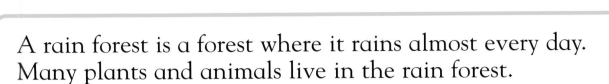

A rain forest is a forest where it rains almost every day. Many plants and animals live in the rain forest.

Color the animals and plants in this picture of a rain forest. Can you name all the animals?

FACTS

Some animals eat only plants. They are called herbivores. Some animals eat only other animals. They are called carnivores.

Circle all of the animals that are herbivores. Point to the animals that are carnivores and say their names out loud.

cow

tiger

crocodile

beaver

horse

deer

Some animals eat both plants and animals.
These animals are called omnivores.

Human beings are omnivores. What do you like to eat?
Draw your favorite food that comes from a plant in the
Plants box. Draw your favorite food that comes from an
animal in the **Animals** box.

What I Like to Eat

Plants

Animals

FACTS

We see with our eyes.

Color the eyes the same as yours. Then write your name beside the picture.

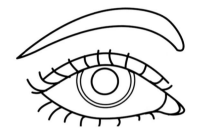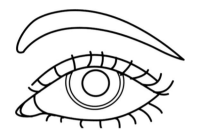

Draw the missing eyes on these animals.

Hot and cold describe the temperature of something. Something that is hot has a high temperature. Something that is cold has a low temperature. A thermometer is used to measure how hot or cold something is.

Point to the pictures of the things that are hot.
Circle the pictures of the things that are cold.

snowman   soup   ice cream

candle flame   ice water   fire

FACTS

We hear with our ears.

Circle the things you can hear with your ears.

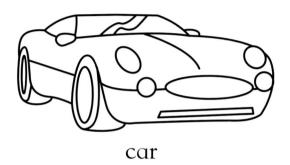

car

book

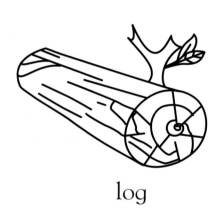

log

bell

cell phone

lamp

A noise can be loud or quiet. If you are close to a noise, it sounds loud. If you are far away from a noise, it sounds quiet.

The dog is barking. Which child hears the dog's bark the loudest? Color that child's shirt red. Which child hears the dog's bark the quietest? Color that child's shirt blue. Then color the whole picture.

FACTS

We use our fingers to feel things. Our fingers tell us if things are hard, soft, rough, smooth, hot, or cold.

TEST **What You Need:**

Gather up a variety of objects from around your house. The objects shown below will work well for this activity, but you can choose others if you like.

tennis ball

orange

wooden spoon

metal spoon

bagel

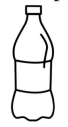
plastic bottle

 What To Do:

1. Ask an adult to help you choose items from around the house.

2. Close your eyes and ask the adult to pass you something.

RESULT

Can you tell what you are holding?
Feel the object and describe it.

We use our nose to smell things.

Circle the things you can smell with your nose.

lemon

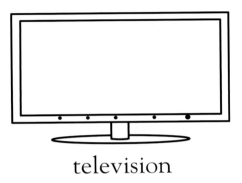

television

garbage

flower

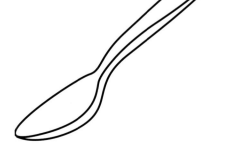

spoon

skunk

FACTS

The nose can detect many different smells.

TEST

What You Need:

1 cup of lemon juice

1 cup of peanut butter

1 cup of vinegar

1 cup of chopped banana

 What to Do:

Close your eyes and ask an adult to pass you a cup to smell. What do you smell? Name the food you are smelling.

RESULT

Put an **X** next to the foods you identified correctly

Peanut butter	
Banana	
Vinegar	
Lemon juice	

We taste food with our tongues.

Foods can taste sweet, salty, or sour. What do these foods taste like? Connect each food to its taste.

lemon

sweet

salty

candy

sour

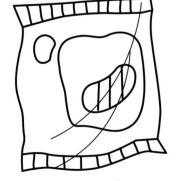

potato chips

FACTS

Animals come in many shapes and sizes.

Animals move in different ways. Some animals walk and run. Some animals swim. Some animals fly. Animals that fly have wings. Circle each animal that has wings.

fly

cat

turtle

bat

bird

fish

Some animals are wild. Other animals can be kept in a house. These animals are tame.

Circle the animals that are wild. Point to the animals that are tame and can be kept in a house.

dog

gorilla

fox

goldfish

hamster

lion

Tame animals can live in your home and be kept as pets.

Do you have a pet?

If you have a pet, what kind of animal is your pet?

What is your pet's name?

Do you have a friend who has a pet?

If you have a friend who has a pet, what kind of animal is that pet?

What is the name of your friend's pet?

Draw your favorite pet.

Pets need special care to keep them happy and healthy.

The pictures below show some of the things pets need to be happy and healthy. Point to the pictures of the things pets need and name them all. Can you think of anything else pets need?

food and water   exercise

home   medical care

home

food and water

exercise

medical care

FACTS

Motion is how things move.

The words in the box describe some of the ways things move. Say the words aloud and point to the picture of the motion each word describes.

| spin | slide | fall | fly | bounce | roll |

bounce

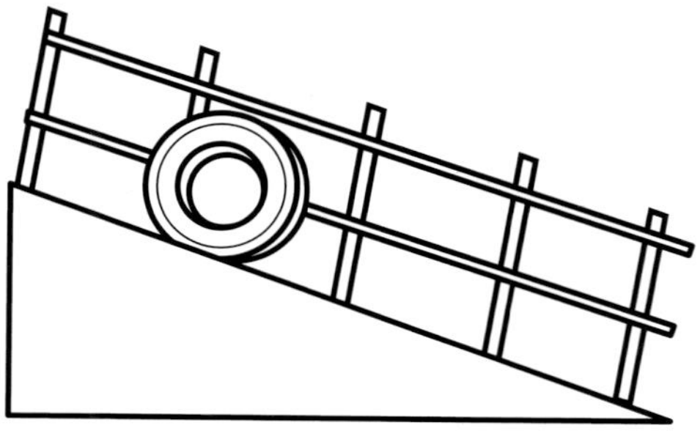

roll

spin

slide

fly

fall

When you move something away from you, you push it.
When you move something closer to you, you pull it.

Look at each picture. Put an **X** in the box to say if the movement shows pushing or pulling.

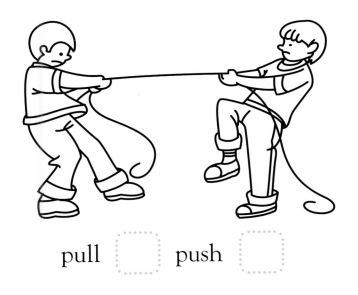

pull ☐   push ☐

pull ☐   push ☐

pull ☐   push ☐

pull ☐   push ☐

Light

Light helps us to see.

Circle the things that generate light.

tree

campfire

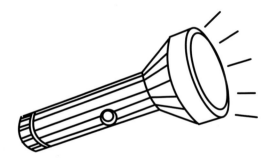

flashlight

sun

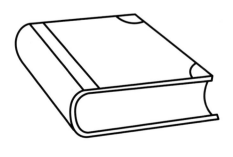

book

lamp

A shadow is a dark patch that forms where an object blocks out light.

TEST

What You Need:

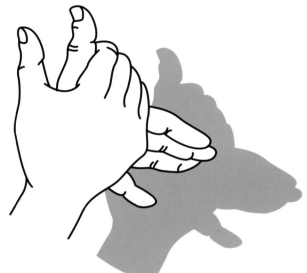

flashlight

**What To Do:**

1. In a dark room, turn on the flashlight and lay it on a table, pointing toward a wall.

2. Stand between the flashlight and the wall. Put your hands together, as shown above, to make the shadow of the dog.

3. What other shadows can you make on the wall?

RESULT

Can you explain what makes the shadow?

A rainbow is an arch of colors that appears when the sun shines through rain.

Color the rainbow.

Red
Orange
Yellow
Green
Blue
Indigo
Violet

You can make a rainbow by shining a light through water.

TEST **What You Need:**

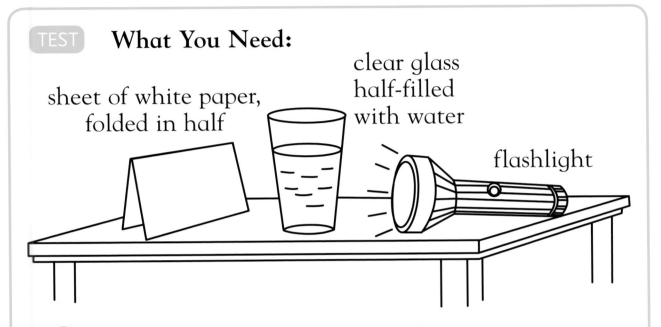

sheet of white paper, folded in half

clear glass half-filled with water

flashlight

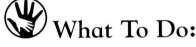 **What To Do:**

1. In a dark room, stand the paper a few inches behind the glass.

2. Turn on the flashlight and shine it through the water onto the paper.

RESULT

What happens? Draw what you see on the paper.

FACTS

The things around you are solids, liquids, or gases.

Solid things keep their shape. Liquid things take the shape of the container they are in. Gases get bigger to fill the space they are in. Circle all the liquids. Point to the solids.

books

candy

juice

balloons

milk

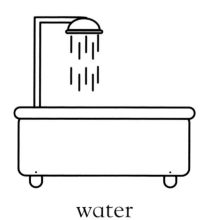

water

Air is a gas. Air is invisible but you can feel it and see that it is there by blowing bubbles.

TEST

What You Need:

drinking straw

glass of water

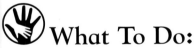 **What To Do:**

1. Blow through the straw. Feel the air coming out of the other end with your hand.

2. Put the straw in the glass of water and blow.

RESULT

Draw what you see happening when you blow through the straw in the water. Why does this happen?

You can fill a balloon with air.

TEST

What You Need:

balloon

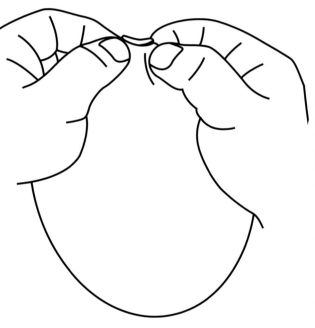

What To Do:

1. Ask an adult to blow into a balloon and fill it with air.

2. Take the balloon in your fingers and hold the mouth firmly to keep the air in.

3. Stretch the mouth of the balloon. Can you hear the air make a squeaky noise as it escapes?

4. Now let go of the balloon.

RESULT

Describe what happened to the balloon. Why do you think this happened?

Wind is moving air.

Draw a circle around the things that use the wind.
Color the picture.

Liquid takes the shape of the container it is in.

TEST

What You Need:

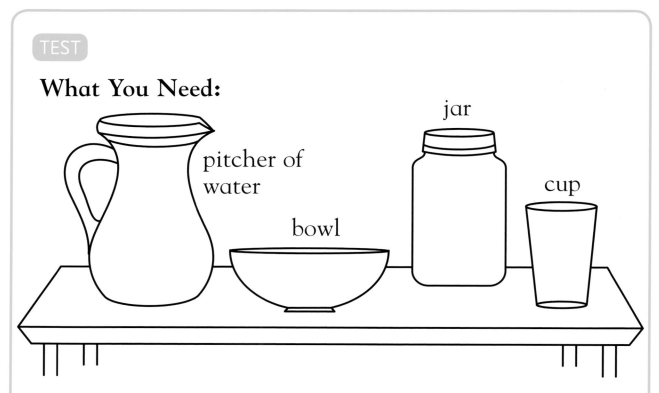

TEST

jar

pitcher of
water

cup

bowl

 What To Do:

1. Pour the water from the pitcher into a cup. See how the water fills the cup and becomes the same shape as the cup.

2. Now pour the water into a bowl. See how the water fills the bowl and becomes the same shape as the bowl.

RESULT

Describe what happens to the water when you pour it into different containers.

FACTS

Bubbles are liquid filled with air.

TEST

What You Need:

2 tablespoons of dish soap

water

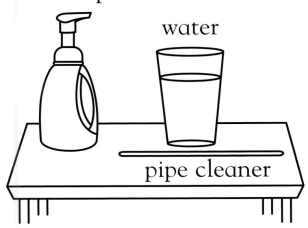

pipe cleaner

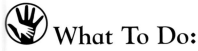 **What To Do:**

1. In a cup, mix together the dish soap and the water.

2. Bend the top of the pipe cleaner into a loop.

3. Dip the pipe cleaner into the bubble mixture and then blow into the loop to make bubbles.

RESULT

Draw what happens.

What is inside the bubbles?

Solids keep their shape.

Draw a line between each object and the shape it matches.

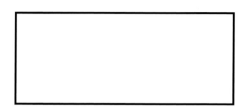

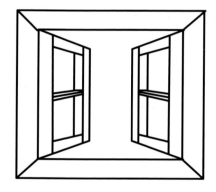

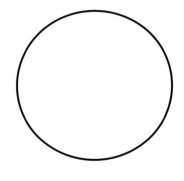

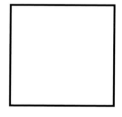

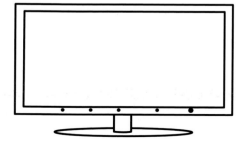

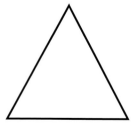

Water can be liquid or solid.

TEST

What You Need:

bowl

water pitcher

ice-cube tray

 What To Do:

1. Pour water into a pitcher. Is this water solid or liquid?

2. Pour the water from the pitcher into an ice-cube tray.

3. Put the ice-cube tray in the freezer for 5 hours.

4. Take the ice-cube tray out of the freezer and put the ice cubes in a bowl. Is the ice solid or liquid?

5. Keep the bowl of ice on a counter overnight. Look at the bowl in the morning.

RESULT

What happened to the water in the freezer?
What happened to the ice in the bowl?

What makes the water change between a solid and a liquid?

Freezing is when a liquid changes into a solid.
Freezing happens when it is very cold.

Look at the pictures. Circle the thing that will freeze in the cold.

juice   book   rain

puddle   car tire   ball

milk   baseball bat   soup

Melting is when a solid turns into a liquid.
Melting happens when it is very warm.

Draw a circle around the objects that melt when it is hot.

apple

book

chocolate

ball

ice cream

sneakers

snowman

hat

bread

Certificate

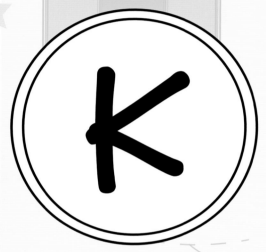

Congratulations to

....

for successfully finishing this book.

GOOD JOB!

You're a star.

Date

....

Answer Section
with Parents' Notes

This book is intended to introduce science concepts to kindergarten children. The topics covered will be similar to the activities they encounter during kindergarten programs.

Contents

By working through this book, your child will practice:
- reading and writing;
- associating pictures and words;
- making observations about the world around him or her;
- categorizing animals and plants by type;
- recognizing habitats;
- finding the differences between types of plants and types of animals;
- performing experiments;
- describing the difference between liquid, solid, and gas;
- using positional words;
- noticing the weather;
- asking questions about what they see.

How to Help Your Child

Kindergarteners will not be able to read most of the instructions in this book—that is understood by the author. Therefore, there is an expectation that parents, guardians, or helpers will work closely with children as they progress through the book. Both parents/helpers and children can gain a great deal from working together.

Perhaps the most important thing you can do—both as you go through the workbook and in many everyday situations—is encourage children to be curious about the world around them. Whenever possible, ask them questions about what they see and hear. Ask them questions such as "Why?," "What if?," and "What do you think?" Do not be negative about their answers, however silly they may be. There is almost certainly a logic to their response, even if it is not correct. Explore and discuss their ideas with them.

Build your child's confidence by praise and encouragement. Celebrate their success.

4

★ Garden

A garden is a small piece of land where flowers, fruits, and vegetables are grown. Some animals live in a garden, too.

Can you find the animals living in the garden? Point to each animal and name it.

A worm, a snail, and a bee are living in the garden.

What other creatures besides those pictured might live in a garden? Explore your own yard or park with your child and discover the plants and animals that live there.

5

Plants ★

A plant has many parts to help it grow.

Find each part of the plant and say its name.

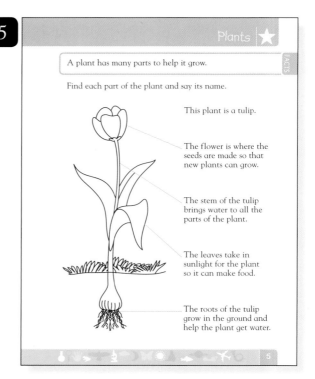

This plant is a tulip.

The flower is where the seeds are made so that new plants can grow.

The stem of the tulip brings water to all the parts of the plant.

The leaves take in sunlight for the plant so it can make food.

The roots of the tulip grow in the ground and help the plant get water.

Some parts of a plant have reproductive functions, others take in water, while others convert sunlight into energy or attract insects to help with pollination. Talk about the role each part plays in keeping the plant healthy.

6

★ Trees

A tree is a large plant. The stem of a tree is made out of wood.

Touch each part of the tree and say its name.
This tree has many of the same parts as the tulip plant you saw on page 5.

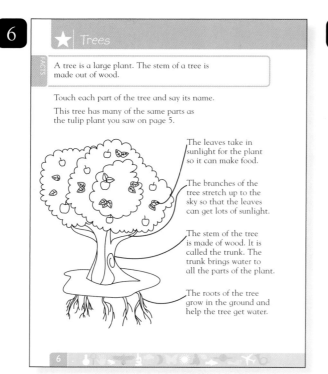

The leaves take in sunlight for the plant so it can make food.

The branches of the tree stretch up to the sky so that the leaves can get lots of sunlight.

The stem of the tree is made of wood. It is called the trunk. The trunk brings water to all the parts of the plant.

The roots of the tree grow in the ground and help the tree get water.

Plants may look very different, but they all have the same parts that perform the same functions. Ask your child to compare the parts of the tulip to the parts of the tree. How are they alike? How are they different?

7

Deciduous Trees ★

Some trees lose their leaves in the fall and grow new leaves in the spring. Trees that lose their leaves are called deciduous trees.

During the summer, deciduous trees have all their leaves. During the fall, the leaves of deciduous trees fall to the ground. During the winter, you only see the branches of a deciduous tree. During the spring, the leaves grow back. Point to each tree and name the season it is in.

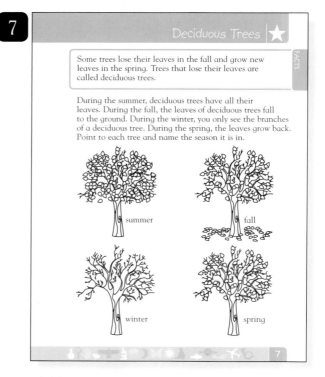

summer

fall

winter

spring

Children of this age will be familiar with the seasonal changes. Discuss how the leaves and trees change with each season and how these and other changes repeat themselves. These patterns of change are called cycles and are part of our environment.

★ Plants We Eat

Many foods that we eat are plants.

Point to the two plants that we eat, and name them.

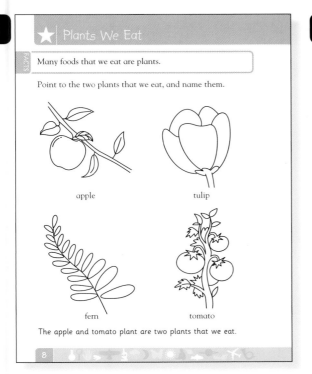

apple

tulip

fern

tomato

The apple and tomato plant are two plants that we eat.

The concept of turning plants into food (i.e., turning tomatoes into tomato sauce) is a difficult one for this age group. A hands-on activity such as cooking can make the concept easier to grasp.

Vegetables ★

Vegetables come from different parts of plants.

The roots of a plant grow in the ground and help the plant get water. Carrots and potatoes are root vegetables. The stem of the plant brings water to all the parts of the plant. Asparagus and celery are stems. The leaves take in sunlight for the plant so it can make food. Spinach and lettuce are leaf vegetables.
Point to each vegetable below, and say its name.
Is it a root, stem, or leaf vegetable?

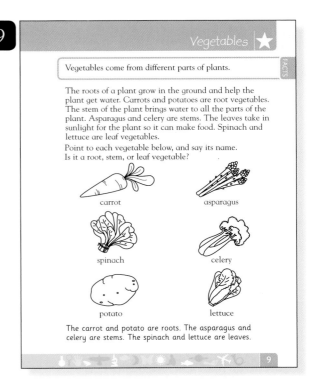

carrot

asparagus

spinach

celery

potato

lettuce

The carrot and potato are roots. The asparagus and celery are stems. The spinach and lettuce are leaves.

Your child will have learned about the different parts of plants and how we use plants for food. This exercise helps to reinforce both of these lessons.

★ Fruits

A fruit is the part of a plant that contains seeds.

Circle the fruit in each picture.

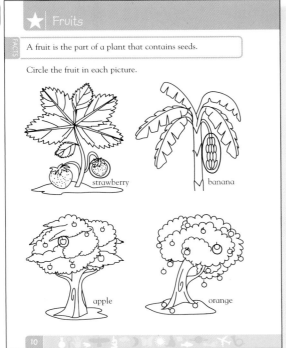

strawberry

banana

apple

orange

All fruits contain seeds, but not all fruits and seeds are easy to identify. Show your child fruits that might not be readily recognized, such as pumpkins and cucumbers, and explain that it is the seeds that make these plants fruit.

Useful Plants ★

Many things we use are made from plants and trees.

Connect each plant with the things that are made from it.

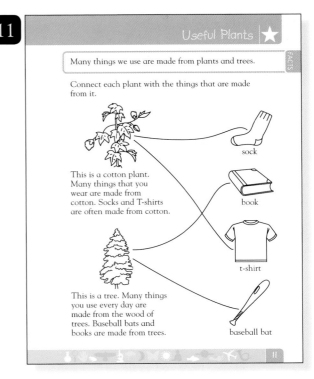

sock

This is a cotton plant. Many things that you wear are made from cotton. Socks and T-shirts are often made from cotton.

book

t-shirt

This is a tree. Many things you use every day are made from the wood of trees. Baseball bats and books are made from trees.

baseball bat

Understanding the concept that many items can be made from trees and plants can be tricky for children. Look for other things around the home that are made from plants and discuss these.

12

★ Plants and Water

FACTS Plants need water to grow.

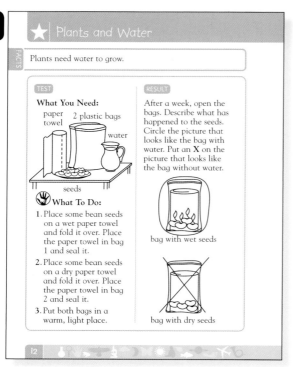

TEST

What You Need:
paper towel   2 plastic bags   water   seeds

✋ **What To Do:**

1. Place some bean seeds on a wet paper towel and fold it over. Place the paper towel in bag 1 and seal it.
2. Place some bean seeds on a dry paper towel and fold it over. Place the paper towel in bag 2 and seal it.
3. Put both bags in a warm, light place.

RESULT

After a week, open the bags. Describe what has happened to the seeds. Circle the picture that looks like the bag with water. Put an **X** on the picture that looks like the bag without water.

bag with wet seeds

bag with dry seeds

Experimentation involves observing, questioning, and sharing. The point of these activities for children is to observe what happens when a plant receives light and water and what happens when it doesn't. Ask the child to predict what will

13

Plants and Light ★

FACTS Plants need light to grow.

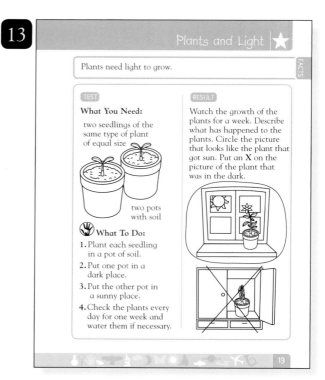

TEST

What You Need:
two seedlings of the same type of plant of equal size

two pots with soil

✋ **What To Do:**

1. Plant each seedling in a pot of soil.
2. Put one pot in a dark place.
3. Put the other pot in a sunny place.
4. Check the plants every day for one week and water them if necessary.

RESULT

Watch the growth of the plants for a week. Describe what has happened to the plants. Circle the picture that looks like the plant that got sun. Put an **X** on the picture of the plant that was in the dark.

happen to each plant. Making predictions is an important part of experimentation. Comparing results to predictions and discussing the experiment's outcome are also key activities.

14

★ Seeds

FACTS Seeds need to travel to different places to grow new plants. They travel to find a place that has light and water.

Seeds travel in many ways. Match the seeds to the way they travel.

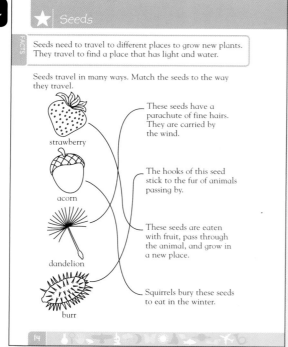

strawberry

acorn

dandelion

burr

These seeds have a parachute of fine hairs. They are carried by the wind.

The hooks of this seed stick to the fur of animals passing by.

These seeds are eaten with fruit, pass through the animal, and grow in a new place.

Squirrels bury these seeds to eat in the winter.

Naming and recognizing the different ways that seeds travel is an excellent way to explain how seeds move to different locations. See if your child can name other seeds that travel in the same way as those listed.

15

Mountains ★

FACTS A mountain is land that rises high above the ground around it. Mountains are made of soil and rocks. Trees grow on some mountains. Very high mountains can be covered in snow.

The animals in the picture live in the mountains. Can you name them all? Color the picture. **Colors may vary**

The animals in the picture are a bear, an eagle, a wolf, and a deer.

Where an animal lives is called a habitat. Children, at this age, are learning about Earth's many habitats. Encourage your child to discuss the wildlife that lives in mountain habitats. Take the opportunity, too, to talk about how mountains are formed.

★ Ocean

An ocean is a large body of water. Ocean water is salty.
Many animals live in the ocean.

Draw a picture of an animal that lives in the ocean.
Then color the picture.
Answers may vary

About 97 percent of the world's water is
contained in the oceans, which have diverse
habitats. Discuss the different zones of the
oceans (sunlit, twilight, and dark) and explain
that different animals live in different zones.

Rain Forest ★

A rain forest is a forest where it rains almost every day.
Many plants and animals live in the rain forest.

Color the animals and plants in this picture of a rain forest.
Can you name all the animals?
Colors may vary

The animals in the picture are a frog, a monkey, a jaguar,
a toucan, and a parrot.

Most rain forests are located near the equator.
Animals and plants that live in them like the hot,
rainy climate. When discussing habitats with your
child, you can talk to them about their own home
and habitat.

★ Herbivores and Carnivores

Some animals eat only plants. They are
called herbivores. Some animals eat only
other animals. They are called carnivores.

Circle all of the animals that are herbivores. Point to the
animals that are carnivores and say their names out loud.

cow

tiger

crocodile

beaver

horse

deer

Continue to discuss the different animals that
are herbivores and those that are carnivores.
Encourage your child to come up with answers
by prompting them with questions such as:
What do sharks eat? What do birds eat? What
do spiders eat?

Omnivores ★

Some animals eat both plants and animals.
These animals are called omnivores.

Human beings are omnivores. What do you like to eat?
Draw your favorite food that comes from a plant in the
Plants box. Draw your favorite food that comes from an
animal in the **Animals** box.
Answers may vary

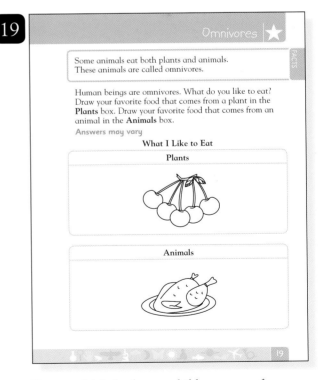

What I Like to Eat

Plants

Animals

Discuss which foods your child eats come from
plants and which foods come from animals.
Some foods, such as cheese and milk, may be
harder for children to identify, so you may
need to prompt them.

★ Sight

We see with our eyes.

Color the eyes the same as yours. Then write your name beside the picture.

Answers may vary

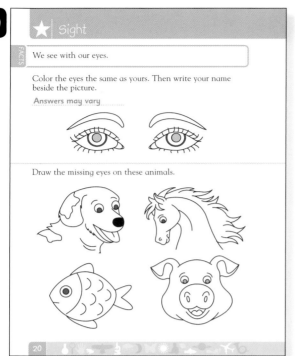

Draw the missing eyes on these animals.

We use our sense of sight to observe our surroundings. Playing a game such as "I Spy" helps children understand how they can see, observe, and describe the world around them.

Hot and Cold ★

Hot and cold describe the temperature of something. Something that is hot has a high temperature. Something that is cold has a low temperature. A thermometer is used to measure how hot or cold something is.

Point to the pictures of the things that are hot.
Circle the pictures of the things that are cold.

snowman   soup   ice cream

candle flame   ice water   fire

Hot and cold can be difficult concepts to describe to children of this age. Using a thermometer to test the temperature of different items to show how hot or cold something is can make this concept easier for children to grasp.

★ Hearing

We hear with our ears.

Circle the things you can hear with your ears.

car   book

log   bell

cell phone   lamp

In this activity your child identified the sounds of objects that make noise. Have them name animals that make sounds and imitate the sound each animal makes.

Volume ★

A noise can be loud or quiet. If you are close to a noise, it sounds loud. If you are far away from a noise, it sounds quiet.

The dog is barking. Which child hears the dog's bark the loudest? Color that child's shirt red. Which child hears the dog's bark the quietest? Color that child's shirt blue. Then color the whole picture.

Some sounds are loud and some are quiet. Play a game with your child in which you each name things that make a loud noise and things that make a quiet noise.

★ Touch

We use our fingers to feel things. Our fingers tell us if things are hard, soft, rough, smooth, hot, or cold.

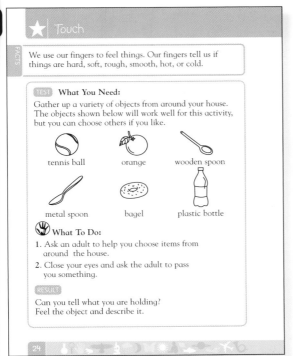

TEST What You Need:

Gather up a variety of objects from around your house. The objects shown below will work well for this activity, but you can choose others if you like.

tennis ball   orange   wooden spoon

metal spoon   bagel   plastic bottle

✋ What To Do:

1. Ask an adult to help you choose items from around the house.
2. Close your eyes and ask the adult to pass you something.

RESULT

Can you tell what you are holding? Feel the object and describe it.

Continue to support your child in this activity by having them not only identify items, but also describe how each object feels. Is it heavy? Smooth? Squishy? Encourage them to use their adjectives.

We use our nose to smell things.

Circle the things you can smell with your nose.

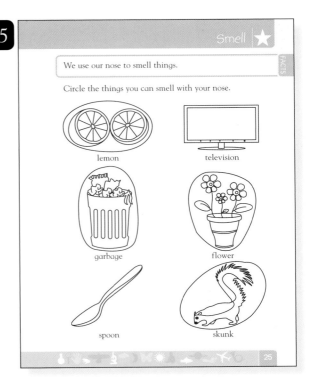

lemon   television

garbage   flower

spoon   skunk

Continue to support your child with this activity by coming up with other things that have a strong smell. What things smell sweet? What things are stinky? Think of different descriptive adjectives.

★ Smell Test

The nose can detect many different smells.

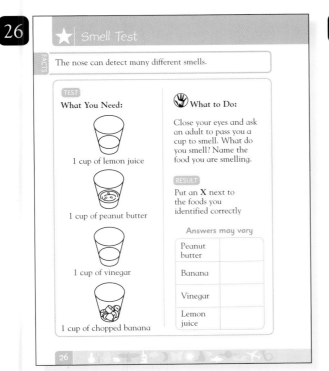

TEST

What You Need:

1 cup of lemon juice

1 cup of peanut butter

1 cup of vinegar

1 cup of chopped banana

✋ What to Do:

Close your eyes and ask an adult to pass you a cup to smell. What do you smell? Name the food you are smelling.

RESULT

Put an **X** next to the foods you identified correctly

Answers may vary

Peanut butter	
Banana	
Vinegar	
Lemon juice	

This science activity is a great way for children to experience how their sense of smell helps them collect information and make scientific observations.

We taste food with our tongues.

Foods can taste sweet, salty, or sour. What do these foods taste like? Connect each food to its taste.

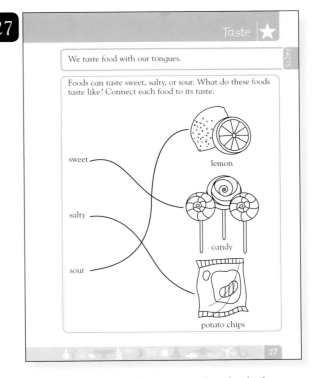

sweet   lemon

salty   candy

sour   potato chips

Encourage your child to name other foods that are sweet, salty, and sour. Which taste do they like the best? Which taste do they like the least?

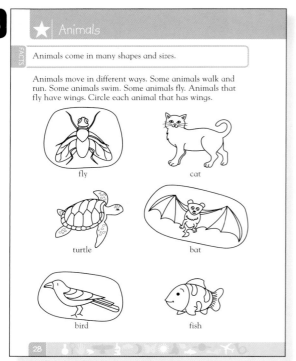

FACTS Animals come in many shapes and sizes.

Animals move in different ways. Some animals walk and run. Some animals swim. Some animals fly. Animals that fly have wings. Circle each animal that has wings.

fly

cat

turtle

bat

bird

fish

Continue learning about how animals get around and move. Name animals that swim. Name animals that walk and run. How do humans move around?

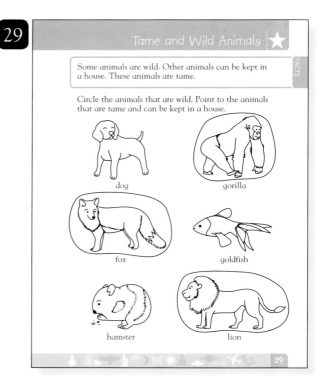

FACTS Some animals are wild. Other animals can be kept in a house. These animals are tame.

Circle the animals that are wild. Point to the animals that are tame and can be kept in a house.

dog

gorilla

fox

goldfish

hamster

lion

Children often know the difference between tame and wild animals at this point. Encourage them to name more wild animals and where these animals live. Also, talk about how wild animals behave differently than tame animals.

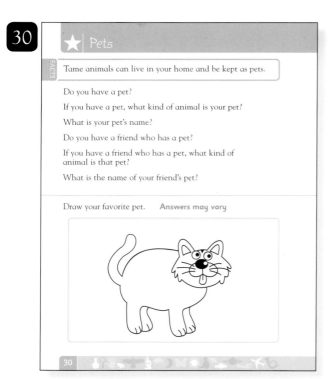

FACTS Tame animals can live in your home and be kept as pets.

Do you have a pet?

If you have a pet, what kind of animal is your pet?

What is your pet's name?

Do you have a friend who has a pet?

If you have a friend who has a pet, what kind of animal is that pet?

What is the name of your friend's pet?

Draw your favorite pet.   Answers may vary

Tame animals live in captivity. Discuss with your child the different homes where tame animals might live: for instance, in a home, in a cage, in a corral.

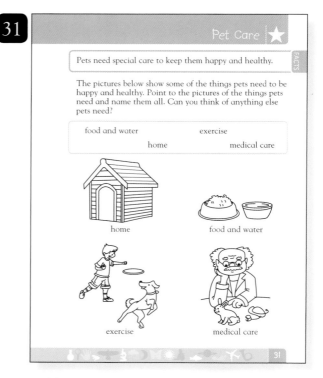

FACTS Pets need special care to keep them happy and healthy.

The pictures below show some of the things pets need to be happy and healthy. Point to the pictures of the things pets need and name them all. Can you think of anything else pets need?

| food and water | exercise |
| home | medical care |

home

food and water

exercise

medical care

Unlike wild animals, which provide their own food and shelter, tame animals rely on humans to take care of them. What other needs do tame animals have? For ex., they need to be bathed. Many of their needs are the same as humans'. Feel free to talk about farm animals as well as pets.

★ Motion

FACTS

Motion is how things move.

The words in the box describe some of the ways things move. Say the words aloud and point to the picture of the motion each word describes.

spin   slide   fall   fly   bounce   roll

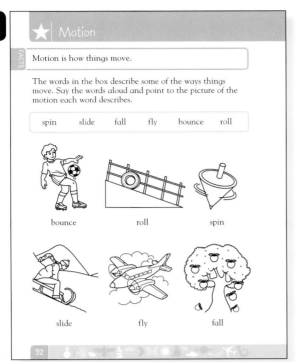

bounce   roll   spin

slide   fly   fall

In addition to the examples given in the exercise, ask your child to name other things that move in the same ways. For ex.: What else can fly? What other objects roll? Can children spin? Collect items from around the house to demonstrate each action.

Pushing and Pulling ★

FACTS

When you move something away from you, you push it. When you move something closer to you, you pull it.

Look at each picture. Put an X in the box to say if the movement shows pushing or pulling.

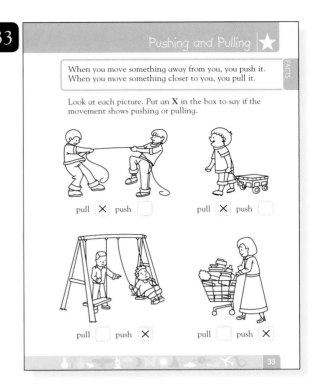

pull [X] push [ ]   pull [X] push [ ]

pull [ ] push [X]   pull [ ] push [X]

An object won't move unless something pushes or pulls on it (a force). A moving object will keep going in a straight line unless something pushes or pulls on it. Have your child push around a ball to demonstrate this concept in a concrete way.

★ Light

FACTS

Light helps us to see.

Circle the things that generate light.

tree   campfire

flashlight   sun

book   lamp

Your child understands that we need light to see. Brainstorm with them and see how many other light sources you can come up with. For ex., the moon, the stars, light bulbs, fireflies, matches, fireworks, and lasers. Draw these on a poster.

Make Shadow Puppets ★

FACTS

A shadow is a dark patch that forms where an object blocks out light.

TEST

What You Need:

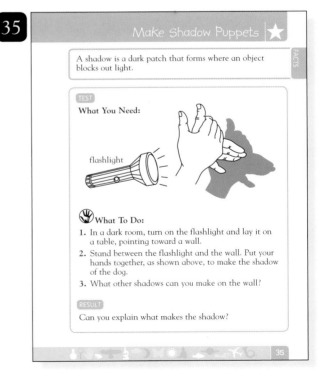

flashlight

✋ What To Do:

1. In a dark room, turn on the flashlight and lay it on a table, pointing toward a wall.
2. Stand between the flashlight and the wall. Put your hands together, as shown above, to make the shadow of the dog.
3. What other shadows can you make on the wall?

RESULT

Can you explain what makes the shadow?

Play outside on a sunny day to show how shadows are made in the sun. Measure your child's shadows at different times of the day—morning, noon, and late afternoon—and discuss how his/her shadow changes. Have your child stand outside on a sunny day and use sidewalk chalk to draw around the shadow they make.

⭐ A Rainbow

A rainbow is an arch of colors that appears when the sun shines through rain.

Color the rainbow.

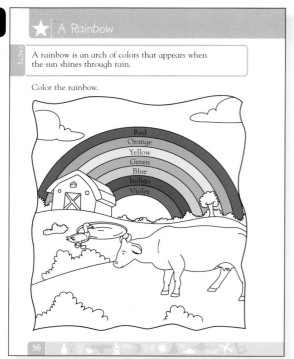

Red
Orange
Yellow
Green
Blue
Indigo
Violet

Try another tactile exercise to illustrate the colors of a rainbow. Use colored candies or colored cereal to create a 3-D rainbow. Glue the candies

Make a Rainbow ⭐

You can make a rainbow by shining a light through water.

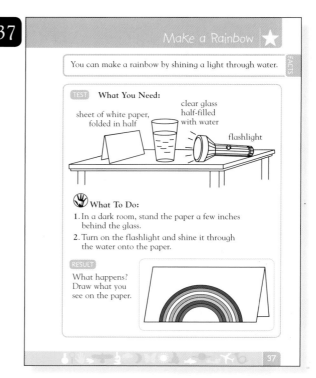

TEST What You Need:

sheet of white paper, folded in half

clear glass half-filled with water

flashlight

✋ What To Do:
1. In a dark room, stand the paper a few inches behind the glass.
2. Turn on the flashlight and shine it through the water onto the paper.

RESULT

What happens? Draw what you see on the paper.

or cereal to a sheet of blue construction paper and have your child say the colors aloud. Here's a trick for remembering the rainbow color order: Roy. G. Biv.

⭐ Solids, Liquids, and Gases

The things around you are solids, liquids, or gases.

Solid things keep their shape. Liquid things take the shape of the container they are in. Gases get bigger to fill the space they are in. Circle all the liquids. Point to the solids.

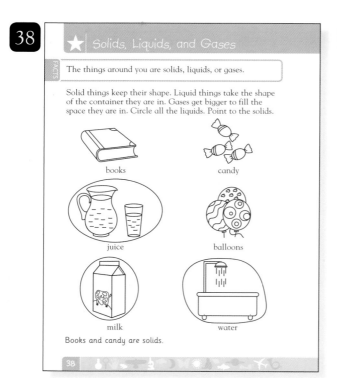

books

candy

juice

balloons

milk

water

Books and candy are solids.

Children this age find it difficult to understand the abstract properties of matter. They will, however, be able to group materials into states like solids and liquids.

Gas ⭐

Air is a gas. Air is invisible but you can feel it and see that it is there by blowing bubbles.

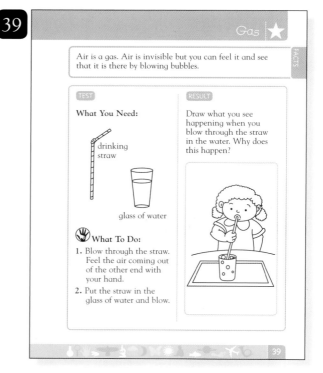

TEST

What You Need:

drinking straw

glass of water

✋ What To Do:
1. Blow through the straw. Feel the air coming out of the other end with your hand.
2. Put the straw in the glass of water and blow.

RESULT

Draw what you see happening when you blow through the straw in the water. Why does this happen?

Hands-on experiments help them identify different forms of matter. Concentrate on shapes and teach them to differentiate forms of matter based on shape. Reinforce the concepts they have already learned.